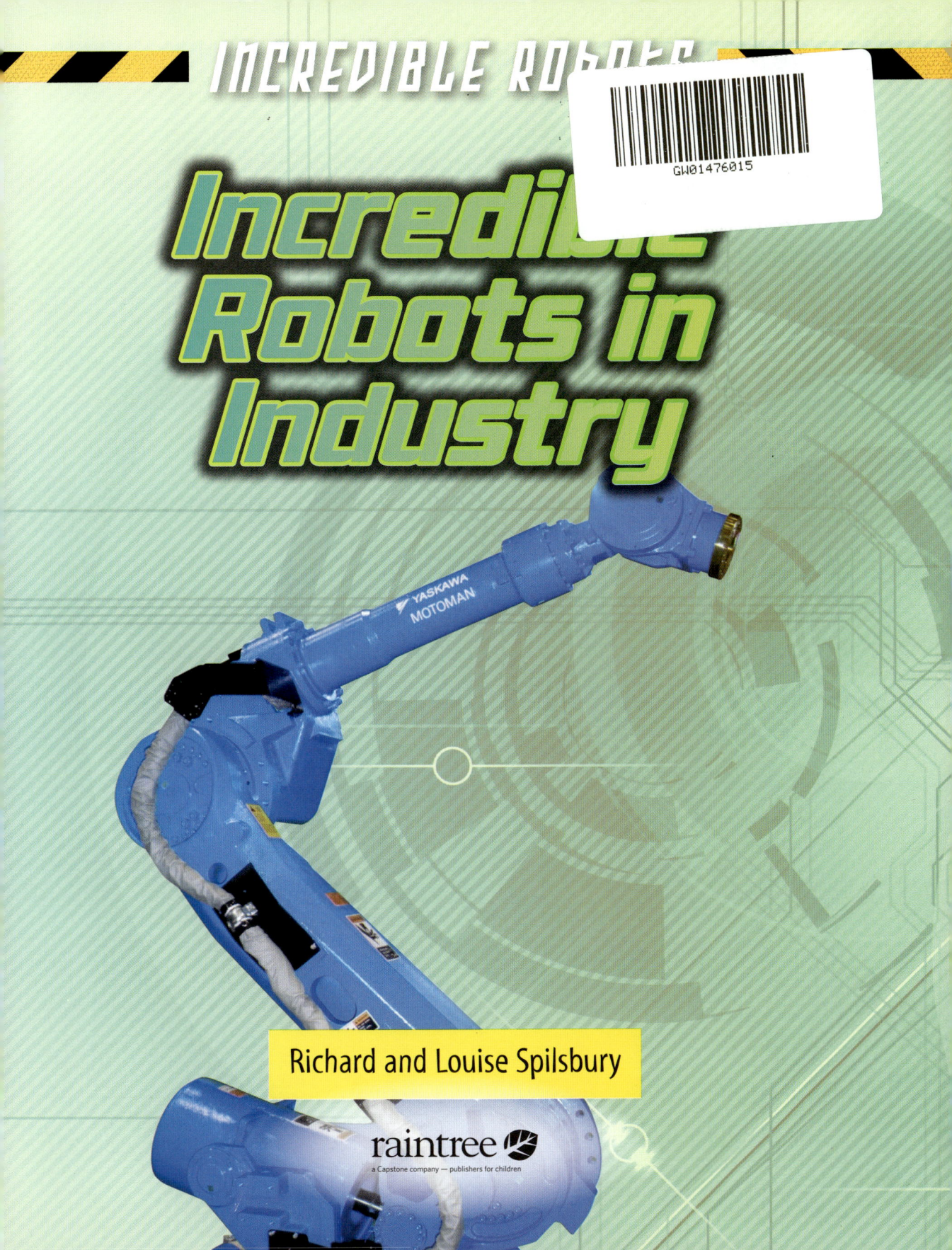

INCREDIBLE ROBOTS

Incredible Robots in Industry

Richard and Louise Spilsbury

raintree
a Capstone company — publishers for children

Raintree is an imprint of Capstone Global Library Limited, a company incorporated in England and Wales having its registered office
at 264 Banbury Road, Oxford OX2 7DY
– Registered company number: 6695582

www.raintree.co.uk
myorders@raintree.co.uk

Text © Capstone Global Library Limited 2017
The moral rights of the proprietor have been asserted.

All rights reserved. No part of this publication may be reproduced in any form or by any means (including photocopying or storing it in any medium by electronic means and whether or not transiently or incidentally to some other use of this publication) without the written permission of the copyright owner, except in accordance with the provisions of the Copyright, Designs and Patents Act 1988 or under the terms of a licence issued by the Copyright Licensing Agency, Saffron House, 6–10 Kirby Street, London EC1N 8TS (www.cla.co.uk). Applications for the copyright owner's written permission should be addressed to the publisher.

Produced for Raintree by Calcium
Edited by Sarah Eason and Amanda Learmonth
Designed by Simon Borrough
Picture research by Susannah Jayes
Production by Victoria Fitzgerald
Originated by Capstone Global Library Ltd © 2016
Printed and bound in India

ISBN 978 1 4747 3125 6 (hardcover)
20 19 18 17 16
10 9 8 7 6 5 4 3 2 1

ISBN 987 1 4747 3203 1 (paperback)
21 20 19 18 17
10 9 8 7 6 5 4 3 2 1

British Library Cataloguing in Publication Data
A full catalogue record for this book is available from the British Library.

Acknowledgements
We would like to thank the following for permission to reproduce photographs: Adept Technology, Inc.: 6l; Agrobot: 40; BMW: 14–15, 16; Dreamstime: Jesse-Lee Lang 4, Guido Vrola 7r; EPRI: 33; Harvet Automation, Inc.: 39; International Climbing Machines (ICM): 34–35; Lely Ireland Ltd: 43; Örebro Universitet: 31; ProKASRO Mechatronik GmbH 36–37; Copyright Rothamsted Research Ltd: 44, 45; Shutterstock: Posmetukhov Andrey 11, Marcin Balcerzak 19, Baloncici 20, 22, 24, Biletskiy 12, Chainfoto24 5, Glovatskiy 32, Nataliya Hora 8, Bob Orsillo 28, RT images 9, Yuyangc 30; Swisslog (UK) Ltd: 21, 25; U.S. Department of Defense: 27; Universal Robots: 17; Copyright WALL-YE: 38; Yaskawa America, Inc.: 1, 6–7, 13.

Cover photographs reproduced with permission of: Shutterstock: Janaka Dharmasena (bg), Amnarj Tanongrattana (fg).

Design Elements by Shutterstock; nice monkey, (stripes) throughout, phipatbig, (robot) throughout, vlastas, (tech background) throughout.

Every effort has been made to contact copyright holders of material reproduced in this book. Any omissions will be rectified in subsequent printings if notice is given to the publisher.

All the internet addresses (URLs) given in this book were valid at the time of going to press. However, due to the dynamic nature of the internet, some addresses may have changed, or sites may have changed or ceased to exist since publication. While the author and publisher regret any inconvenience this may cause readers, no responsibility for any such changes can be accepted by either the author or the publisher.

Contents

Chapter 1 4
Robots in factories

Chapter 2 10
Robot production

Chapter 3 18
Robot warehouse

Chapter 4 26
Hazardous conditions

Chapter 5 32
Robot inspectors

Chapter 6 38
Robot farming

Glossary 46

Find out more 47

Index 48

Chapter 1
Robots in factories

In 1959, a new type of worker started a test shift at the General Motors vehicle factory in New Jersey, USA. This was the first factory robot **prototype**, called *Unimate*. *Unimate* was a huge and heavy machine that completed tasks that were difficult for people to do, including removing and stacking very hot metal disks. For a while the vehicle industry was the only industry to use robots in its factories. However, since that time, industrial robots have become far more complicated and capable, and they are a feature in most major factories in the world.

Could robots like this be the factory workers of the future?

Made for robots

A robot is any automatically operated machine that can be used to do work that is usually performed by humans. The jobs done in a factory are often dull and repetitive, making factory work ideal for robots. In a factory, items are produced on a **production line**, where a car or other item, such as a television, moves along a **conveyor belt** or assembly line. At different stopping points, the same part is attached to machine after machine. Doing a repetitive job like this can be tiring and boring. Another problem is that when humans get tired or bored, they can easily make mistakes. People can work for only a certain number of hours before they need a break or time off. Robots can work 24 hours a day for years on end, doing exactly the same job in exactly the same way every time, without fail. A robot can be programmed once and then repeat exactly the same task for years.

Robots can do jobs that are too dull, dirty or dangerous for humans to do.

Keeping people safe

Another advantage of robots is that they can do jobs, such as handling hot metal or working on hazardous cutting machines, which are dangerous for humans to do. Instead of putting humans at risk of injury or death, factory owners are able to use machines that can be repaired if they are broken. Robots can also be stronger, faster and more efficient than humans. A robot the size of a person can easily carry a load far heavier than a human ever could, and can be programmed to do repetitive tasks far more quickly.

The word "robot" comes from the Czech word *robota*. This translates into English as "forced labour".

Types of arms

There are many types of industrial robots. These robots may be similar in some ways, but one of the most basic differences is in their arms. Robot arms are the industrial robot's most important part, because tools for specific jobs can be attached to the arms. Robot arms have **joints**, where two parts bend and move in different directions. Most joints are moved by powerful electrical motors but some operate using **hydraulics**.

Sliding arms

A Cartesian robot is a **stationary** robot that can move its arm in a straight line but cannot rotate it. It has three sliding joints to move its "wrist" up and down, in and out, or backwards and forwards. These robot arms are used for jobs such as applying glue to a precise spot on a product, time after time.

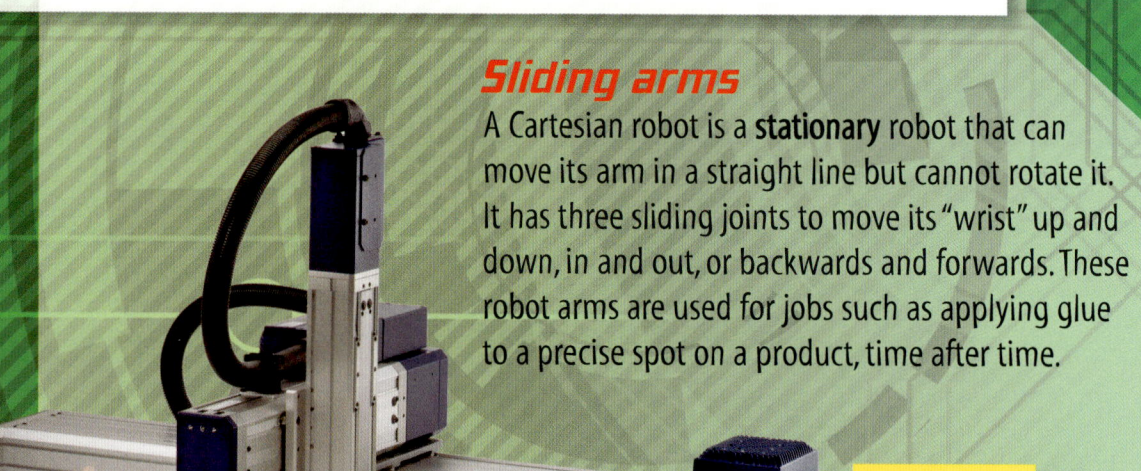

The *Python* is an example of a Cartesian robot.

Three joints

Some robot arms have three joints, each rotating in the same plane or direction. Each joint rotates in the same way as a shoulder or hip joint. These robot arms provide a wider range of movement than the Cartesian arms. They are often used to pick and place objects in boxes, or to handle tools.

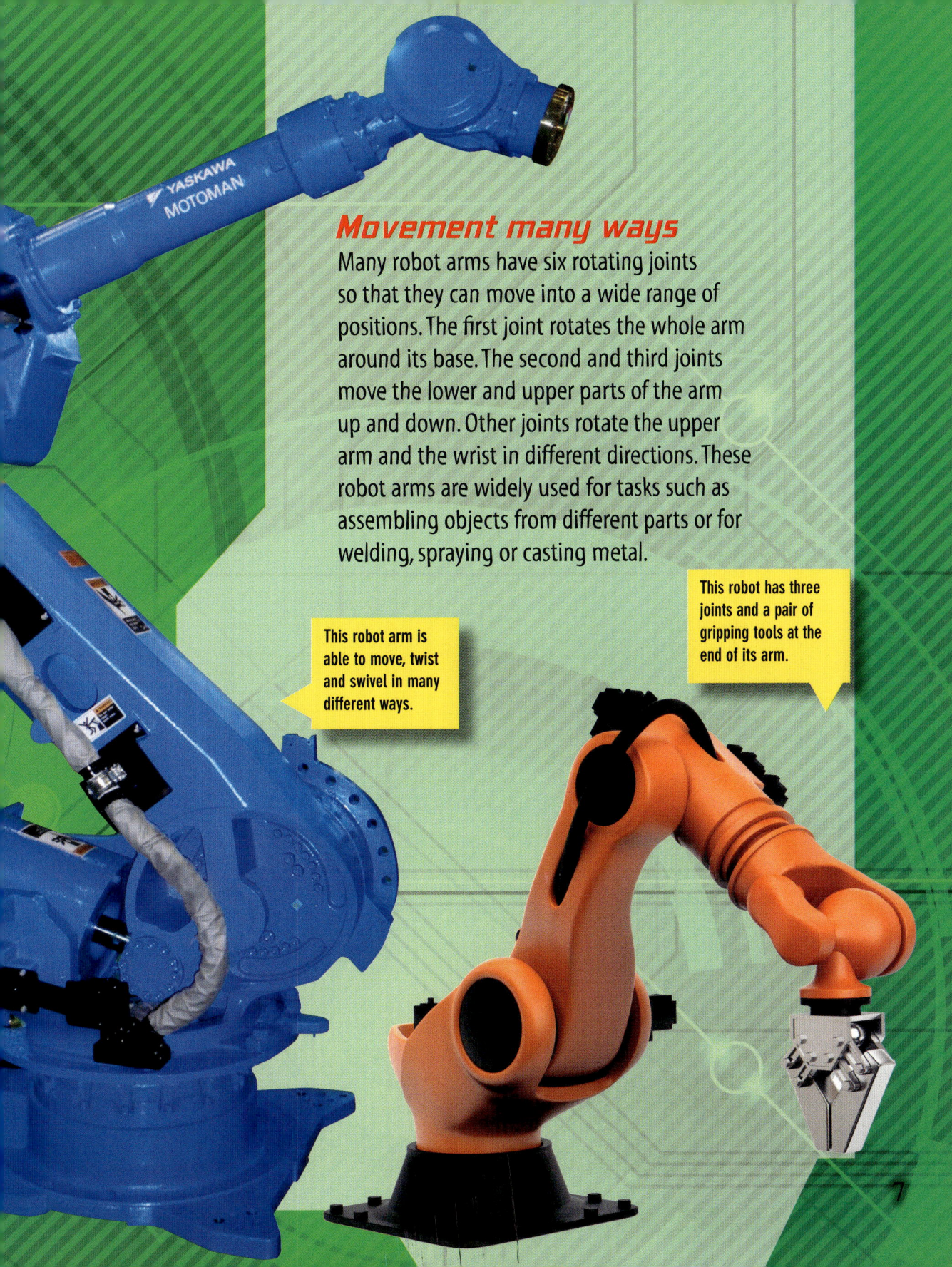

Movement many ways

Many robot arms have six rotating joints so that they can move into a wide range of positions. The first joint rotates the whole arm around its base. The second and third joints move the lower and upper parts of the arm up and down. Other joints rotate the upper arm and the wrist in different directions. These robot arms are widely used for tasks such as assembling objects from different parts or for welding, spraying or casting metal.

This robot arm is able to move, twist and swivel in many different ways.

This robot has three joints and a pair of gripping tools at the end of its arm.

Industrial uses

Different robots are designed to do different jobs. Some robots are large and heavy with strong arms to lift things, while others are smaller, more nimble and capable of fine, intricate work. To do these jobs, the robot's arms are equipped with a wide range of **end effectors**. Some end effectors look a little like simple human hands, with fingers that grasp and grip objects. These end effectors may have built-in **sensors** to detect how much **pressure** the hand is using to do its task. The sensors make sure that the hand does not cause damage. For example, if a robot hand that screws plastic lids onto bottles crushes each lid, it is wasteful, time consuming and makes industrial processes inefficient. Other end effectors are types of tools, such as soldering irons, drills, spanners and paint-spraying nozzles.

Robots are widely used for all kinds of work in vehicle factories.

Some robots can do intricate work, such as installing computer chips in electrical products.

Robots at work

Robots are used across a wide range of industries, from the vehicle and aviation industries to farming and warehousing. Robots are important for making the computers we rely on, not just to write papers or do research on the internet, but also to control a wide range of devices, from smartphones and microwave ovens to refrigerators, vehicles and even other robots! Fine-scale end effectors on robot arms can solder tiny wires to **silicon chips**, position **components** onto printed **circuit boards**, and make and cut up the silicon crystals used to make the chips.

Robots are used in the food and pharmaceutical industries, too. When you open a box of sweets and it is perfectly arranged by colour, that is often the work of robot hands, gently lifting and placing sweets in the right place in the assortment. Drugs and medicines are packed in their capsules and other containers by robot arms in pharmaceutical factories.

Chapter 2
Robot production

In the early 20th century, Henry Ford invented the assembly line for his vehicle plant. Workers stayed in one place and did one job, such as bolting on a door. Wheeled trolleys were used to carry the partly finished car from one worker to the next. Ford's assembly line cut the time for assembling a car from 12 hours to 90 minutes and, as a result, reduced the price by two-thirds! Today, the workers on parts of many vehicle and aeroplane assembly lines are robots.

Start-up costs

Robots are expensive to buy, and it also costs a lot to train people to use them. However, as assembly-line workers, robots have several advantages over human workers:

▶ Robots can keep going for 24 hours a day, seven days a week, stopping only now and then to be oiled, checked and repaired.

▶ Robots can be built to be much stronger than people. They never get tired or risk injuring themselves by lifting heavy objects.

▶ Robots can operate in hazardous working conditions, such as in areas with strong chemical fumes or high temperatures.

▶ Robots deliver consistent results every time they carry out a task.

At exhibitions like this one, manufacturers can see the advantages of using robots to do factory work!

Saving money

Robots can help companies manufacture things faster and more cheaply. This means that companies can produce more goods to sell at lower prices. For example, the aircraft manufacturer Boeing is planning to speed up production of aeroplanes to meet global orders by adding more robots to its factory. Robot arms can put a coat of paint on a plane wing in 24 minutes, while a human would take four hours to paint the same wing. A robot can also drill holes to join parts of the plane body with 93 per cent more accuracy than humans.

Robots are the future

According to one study, in the near future, the use of robots in industry could create up to 1.5 million new jobs! There could be new job opportunities to engineer, program, train, maintain and repair the robots. In many cases, companies are using robots so that they can expand and improve product quality and increase production. Companies will end up hiring more people, such as engineers and sales staff, to support that growth. However, some people think that nearly half of all employees in some countries are in jobs that could be done by robots. Many fear that this could put people out of work and make it even harder for them to make a living.

Welding

Welding is what happens when different pieces of metal are heated to very high temperatures so that they melt together. As the metal cools and hardens, the different pieces of metal join together and you often cannot see the point at which they were joined. In addition to being burnt or hit in the eyes by sparks when handling hot metal, human welders can become ill from the fumes given off by the melting metal. Workers do wear protective clothing and masks to keep safe, but welding is a job that many factories leave to robots.

Human welders have to wear protective clothing and equipment to prevent them being injured while working.

Taking the heat

Factories that produce products with metal bodies must weld parts together. To melt steel, electricity heats metal devices called **electrodes**. The electrodes are used to weld metal parts at very precise locations in a process called spot welding. When robots spot-weld, electricity flows into the electrodes at the end of a robot arm. The electrodes squeeze the pieces together and heat up and melt the steel where the parts need to be joined. At that precise spot, the metals mix, and when they cool, they harden.

Spot welding can be used to join the metal parts that form the chassis (body) of a car to the floor panel, or the engine compartment and the roof panel to the side panels. Welding can also be used on thinner metals such as those used to make the exterior of aircraft wings.

Super-efficient robots

Using a robot for welding increases **productivity**. For example, a human welder can keep a hot torch on an object for about 30 per cent of the time they are working on it, while a robot can do so for at least 90 per cent of the time. Also, the welding that robots do is accurate and consistent. This kind of accuracy means no material or time is wasted, and this also saves factories money.

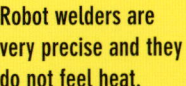

Robot welders are very precise and they do not feel heat.

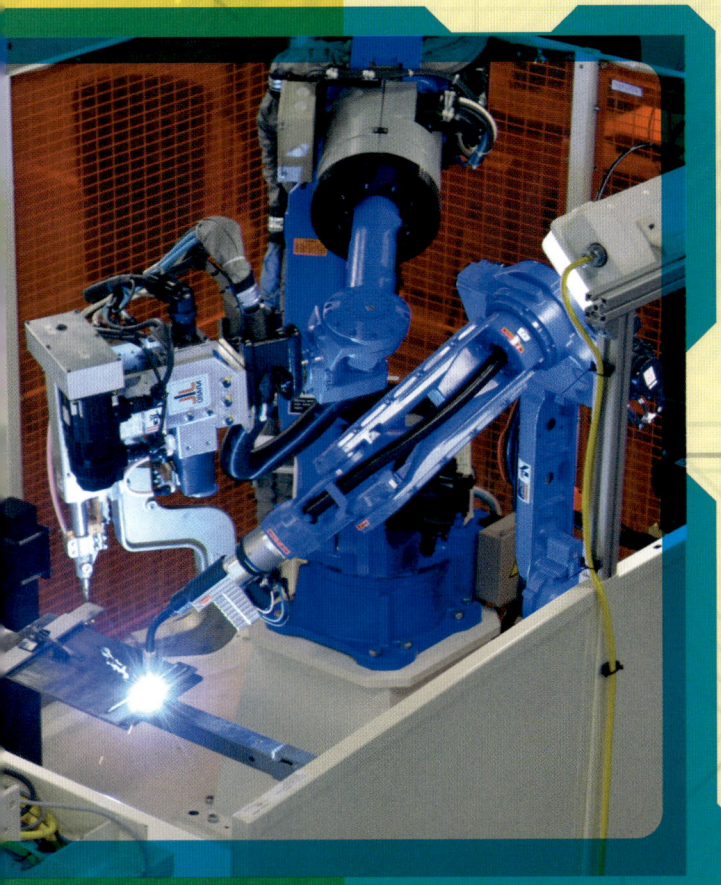

Robots are the future

In the future, robot arms could use **lasers** to weld objects together. Laser welding uses light beams to create very accurate, narrow and deep holes. The end result is better because the joins are less visible. Laser welding causes less surface damage to metals.

13

Painting

Robot arms tipped with spray nozzles connected by pipes to drums of paint can be used to spray-paint metal parts of vehicles. Each vehicle typically has five coats of paint, with a combined thickness of five human hairs. The paintwork of a vehicle includes coatings to prevent **corrosion** of the metal, and colour and sealant to stop paint from fading in the sun. Each coat is dried before the next layer goes on.

Programmed to paint

Operators program painting robots using computer 3D models of vehicles. This works out to be the most time- and cost-effective way of painting vehicle shells. It also means that the coats of paint are the right thickness, are even, and do not have any unsightly drips, bubbles or ripples. The chemicals used in paints are hazardous for humans to inhale and can cause illnesses such as breathing problems and **cancers**. The paints are also **flammable**, so they could explode. Painting robots do their work in sealed rooms to keep any hazards contained. The rooms are also flameproof, so if there is a fire, the rooms will not be destroyed.

Painting team

In some vehicle factories, there are teams of painting robots. Three-joint robots with rubber-tipped fingers or hooks open, hold and close bonnets and doors. Programmers use computers to coordinate the movements with six-joint or seven-joint robots that paint the surfaces. The painting robots can rotate joints to reach into every part of a vehicle shell and also on all sides of components for use later on the assembly line. The robot teams are often mounted on rails so that they can move along the length of vehicles, making sure that all surfaces are properly painted.

In many factories, two or more painting robots work on one vehicle at the same time.

Robots are the future

Vehicles are not the only things that will be painted by robots in the future. A robotic painter called *e-David* is creating fine art paintings. *e-David* has built-in cameras to take a photograph of a person or object, which it then converts into a unique sequence of brushstrokes using computer software. It then uses a gripper to pick up different-sized brushes and dip them into paint to build up a painting. The robotic painter can repeat a subject but its brushstrokes are never identical. Could galleries of the future be stocked with robot paintings?

Finishing

At the end of the vehicle assembly line, parts of the interior and exterior trim are glued, clipped and bolted together. Engines, seats, instruments, steering wheels, tyres, glass and many other parts are combined with the chassis to make finished cars. In the past, the end of the vehicle assembly line was the one part of the line where fewer robots were used. However, today things are changing, and more and more robots are being used to help at the end of the line, too.

Never tired

Robots are tireless workers. They tighten bolts with the right amount of force so that the engines are firmly attached to the chassis. They attach seals accurately on the inside of doors to keep out sound and rain, and they lift heavy parts into place for attaching time after time, no matter how many hours they have been working. However, there are thousands of parts, some very small, used in the final finishing, so it is difficult to program robots to do everything. Humans are still needed … for now!

Robots can be used to help human workers do some of the lifting necessary in their job.

Robot powers

Human workers can easily be injured during vehicle finishing. For example, they may strain their arms or back through repeated movements, such as bolting parts together or lifting heavy objects.

Robots are the future

A new **humanoid** robot called *Baxter* has been designed to work alongside people, for example, in assembling cars or packaging items from a conveyor belt. *Baxter* can learn new tasks by moving its arms through the sequence of movements required to perform the task. The robot's built-in computer memory stores the sequence, and then repeats it, time after time, without getting bored or straining itself.

Sensors in the robot are used to track human movements, so *Baxter* avoids bumping into people and moves out of their way. In the future there may be many more of these robots that do not require special programming to learn jobs. They may find work in many industries as part of a mixed human/robot team!

Robots such as this one are used to help assemble cars in manufacturing plants.

This is why some manufacturers are giving their workers robot powers. The Equipois X-Ar™ is an **exoskeleton** arm, supported on the ground, which attaches to the outside of a human arm. The exoskeleton supports the weight of the human arm using powered joints, making it easier for people to work for longer with their arms outstretched.

17

Chapter 3

Robot warehouse

Warehouses are buildings where goods and products are delivered and stored until a customer orders them. Some warehouses are fairly small and contain only one type of product. Others can be bigger than 14 football pitches put together! A huge variety of goods, from books and bowls to televisions and tools, can be stored at a warehouse. People who work in warehouses do a wide range of jobs, such as taking delivery of goods and supplies, checking for damaged or missing items, moving stock around by using lifting gear or a forklift, picking and packing orders, and loading goods. Many warehouses use robots to do some or all of these jobs.

Moving goods around

Some warehouses use conveyor-belt systems to move goods around. These look a little like the baggage reclaim carousels you find at airports. In a warehouse, there can be hundreds of conveyor belts working together to carry goods from one area of the warehouse to another. When a product arrives at a warehouse, it is **scanned** into a computer system and given a number or **barcode**. Later, when a customer orders the product, it is picked, packed and placed on a conveyor belt that moves it from its storage area to a point of collection. There, it will be picked and loaded onto a delivery vehicle and taken to the customer.

> Conveyor belts can even move delicate eggs around safely without them rolling, falling or crashing into each other!

Computer control

The conveyor-belt system is linked to a computer that knows exactly what specific area or delivery truck the product should be sent to. As the product moves along on one conveyor belt, it will suddenly be dropped onto a belt going in another direction, at just the right moment. Finally, the system will drop it off right where it is supposed to be! If there is a problem, for example, if a belt breaks down or a package becomes stuck, human controllers can use closed-circuit television (**CCTV**) cameras to see what is wrong. They can solve the problem, usually by tweaking the program.

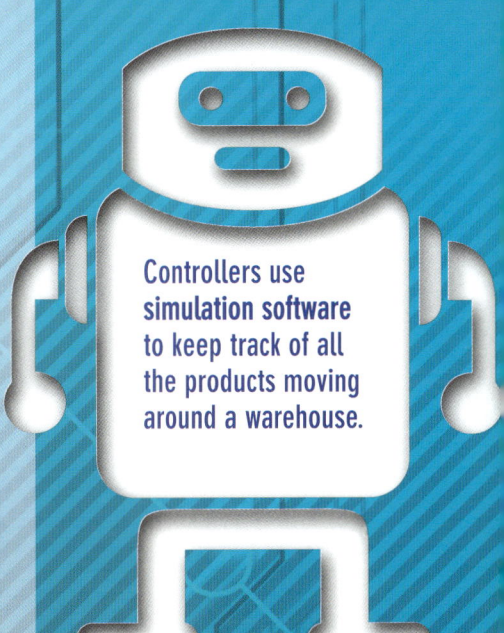

Controllers use **simulation software** to keep track of all the products moving around a warehouse.

Pickers

Items must be picked, or selected, and packaged before being placed onto a conveyor belt. This can take human workers a long time to do, so many warehouses use hundreds of **autonomous** robots operated by control software to speed up this process.

Perfect pickers

In the past, human workers used to walk along stacks of shelves to pick up products for orders and then return to a workstation to put that product into a box and send it to its next destination. Today, many warehouses use small Kiva or similar robots to do this job. These robots can race along the aisles, picking up goods and carrying them to humans at their workstations. At their workstations, the workers will sort and package them.

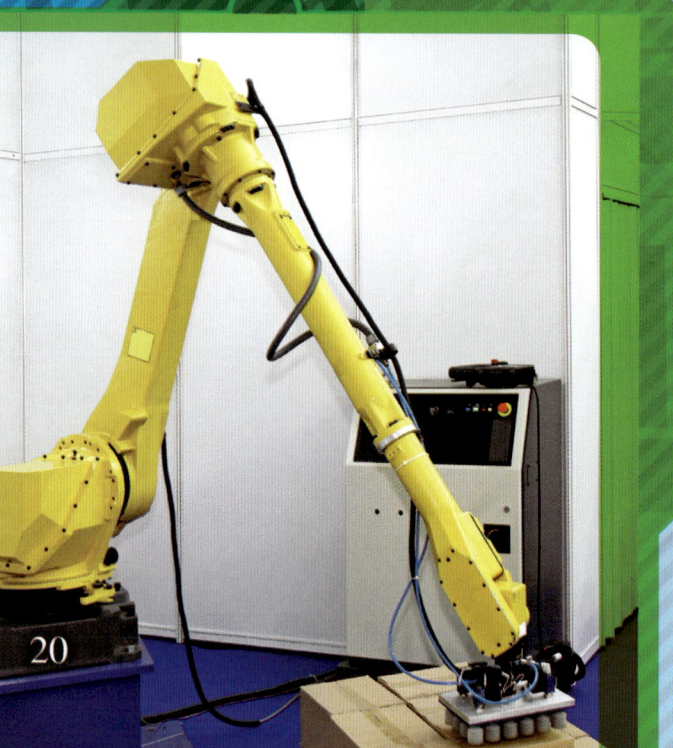

This robotic arm is used for packing items in a warehouse.

In some larger warehouses, where human pickers would have to walk down very long aisles to get items, the average length of time it takes to collect an order from a shelf and place it in a box has been reduced from about 90 minutes to about 15 minutes! As well as saving time, there are additional space-saving advantages. Shelves can be placed closer together because robots are smaller than the trolleys people had to push down the wide aisles.

Ground-based robots that pick and carry products enable companies to deliver millions more items to customers every day.

How it works

When an order is received, a computer calculates which robot is nearest the item requested, and sends that robot to collect it. By following a series of computerized barcode stickers on the floor, the robot finds its own way to the shelf unit where the item is stored. When the robot arrives at the shelf, it drives beneath the object and lifts it off the ground, before carrying it to a human worker at a workstation. As the robots zoom around the warehouse floor, sensors ensure that they avoid bumping into each other. The sensors tell the robot when another robot or other obstacle is near, so that the robot can take a slightly different path.

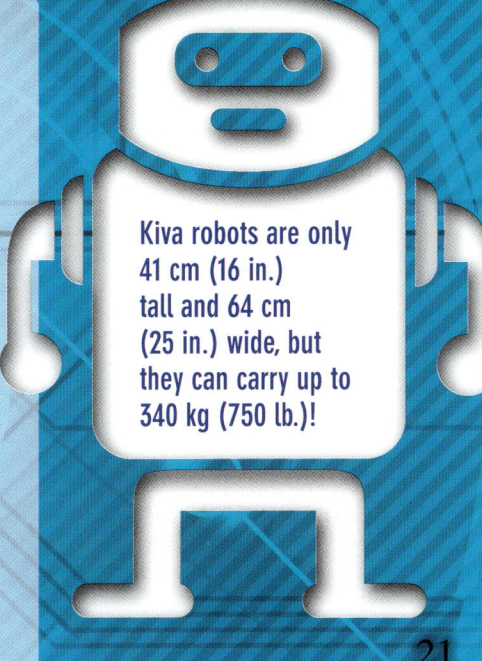

Kiva robots are only 41 cm (16 in.) tall and 64 cm (25 in.) wide, but they can carry up to 340 kg (750 lb.)!

Space-saving robots

There are other types of robot systems that can help companies store and collect goods from different sites in a warehouse. AutoStore is a space-saving system for storing and picking single items and small parts or cases. It is used in different types of warehouses, but in particular in the food, drink and pharmaceutical industries.

Automated storage warehouses save companies space, time and money.

Control centre

AutoStore robots lift and deliver crates of goods to stations, controlled by a smart central system. The difference between this system and other collection systems is that instead of driving along the ground between shelf units, the autonomous Autostore robots operate on a 3D metal grid. The items in the warehouse are stored in crates within a high aluminium grid system. The robots automatically store and retrieve goods from the grid and carry them to a person at a workstation. The robots move along a rail on the grid. Each robot stays at the top of the grid, using an extendable lifting tool with four steel bands to grab and lift crates from within each stack of crates in the grid. The robots have sensors near their wheels to sense where they are on the rail. This information is sent to the warehouse control system, which can track the robots' locations.

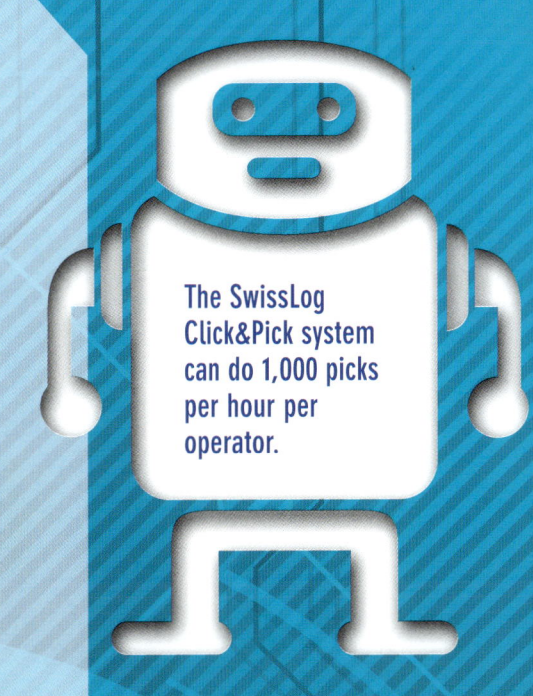

The SwissLog Click&Pick system can do 1,000 picks per hour per operator.

Faster and fewer mistakes

As well as being faster than human workers, using the robots makes it unlikely that the wrong items will be picked. Another advantage is that items can be stored very closely together – up to 60 per cent more goods can be stored in the same area of a more traditional warehouse. This kind of space saving means that there could be more warehouses in city centres. City warehouses would save time and transport costs in bringing goods from giant out-of-town warehouses.

Distribution

After items have been picked from a storage site in a warehouse, a conveyor belt may move them to the distribution section. From there they are loaded onto **pallets** and into delivery trucks. Using the latest robot technology, many warehouses have systems of robots to load goods onto pallets. These robots can lift and load complete pallets of goods carefully and accurately, to stack a complete unit load.

Super-smart robots

Some robots are programmed to load boxes or other packages onto a pallet in a particular pattern, to ensure that the items are stacked safely and to fit the maximum number of units on each pallet. Many of these robots are in a fixed position and have special tools designed for the specific items they load, for example, bottles or boxes of delicate fruit and vegetables.

One advantage of using robots to load pallets is that they can lift and load large, bulky packages safely and efficiently.

These robots use the grippers on the tool at the end of their arm to grasp and pick up items from one moving conveyor belt, and swiftly and gently place them onto a pallet on another moving conveyor belt heading for a distribution truck nearby.

Independent robots

Modern loading robots can move independently. These automated guided vehicle (AGV) systems look rather like robot forklifts. They usually move around by following markers or wires on the warehouse floor. They can locate, lift and extract pallets of goods from shelves or other locations, and transport them to the distribution section.

AGVs like this one can move autonomously around a factory floor.

Some AGVs autonomously attach themselves to trailers that hold products and then tow the trailer behind them to their destination. Lasers guide other AGVs, so this saves the warehouse from having to put markers or wires on the floor. These AGVs have laser beams that calculate the robot's position by reflecting lasers off mirrors located around the work area.

Robots are the future

In the future, there may be swarm AGVs in warehouses. Like a colony of ants or bees controlled by a single queen, these AGVs would work autonomously while still being linked to all the other robots and coordinated by a central computer.

Chapter 4
Hazardous conditions

One of the most important reasons for using robots is to prevent people from working in hazardous environments and from handling dangerous materials. Robots are in demand in a wide range of industries. In some industries the hazard is obvious. For example, in the arms and chemicals industries, workers may be making products containing potentially **lethal** substances. **Missiles** may contain some of the most explosive substances on Earth, and robot arms take on the work of handling these substances, packing and transporting completed missiles in factories. In the chemicals industry, robot arms may handle strong acids and other harmful substances.

Hidden dangers
In other industries the hazards are not so obvious. For example, explosions can happen in cement and flour warehouses. As powders, cement and flour can explode when dust combines with oxygen in the air. For this reason, robot arms are used to fill flour and cement bags. To reduce the possibility of a blaze, the air in the filling room has **nitrogen** pumped into it, because nitrogen prevents fires.

Industrial pollution
Many industries release chemicals into the environment, often by accident. Some chemicals, such as lead and mercury, are highly poisonous and can threaten the health of many living things. Robots are used to locate

pollution and in some cases, clear it up. The robots are autonomous remote vehicles (ARVs) that move on wheels or **caterpillar tracks**, and are operated by people using remote-control handsets. Arms on these robots can be fitted with specialized tools, for example, sensors to detect problem chemicals, and shovel attachments to take soil samples or clear **contaminated** soil from an area.

Robots are the future

In the future, building in hazardous places, such as reconstruction after earthquakes or building settlements on planets with no air, could be left to teams of robots. Scientists have created small robots with simple intelligence based on that of termites, which together build remarkable mounds in which to live. The termite-bots carry and lay bricks and climb the structures they build together to reach the next laying site. They build following simple rules, such as moving only in particular directions so that they do not bump into each other, and checking the surrounding bricks before laying the next one.

ARVs have arms that can be used to remove hazardous materials or dangerous devices.

Nuclear power

Nuclear power is an important energy resource, supplying around 15 per cent of global electricity. The electricity is generated using heat produced by nuclear fuel in a **reactor**. During use, the fuel changes into nuclear waste that is highly hazardous. The waste produces **radiation**, which includes invisible gamma rays that can pass through and affect normal body tissue. It also produces radioactive particles that are hazardous when breathed in or swallowed. In the nuclear industry, waste is either stored for long periods underwater or in tough concrete vessels until it becomes less radioactive or is reprocessed into nuclear fuel. Workers are at risk when working with nuclear waste, either in the plants themselves or outside at storage facilities.

Human workers dealing with hazardous substances must wear protective suits and masks to keep themselves safe.

Robots and radiation

To protect workers in the nuclear industry, robots are widely used. They are designed with instruments and working parts that are unaffected by radioactivity. Robot arms are used to lift and carry nuclear waste into storage. They are used to put nuclear fuel into reactors and handle the rods that are important in controlling the nuclear reaction. Some robots are large arms with gripper hands to pick up things. Others are narrow, snake-like arms that can twist into small openings to make repairs to pipes and other reactor parts, using drills, cutters, grippers and other tools.

When radiation is present, Geiger counters click. Rapid clicks mean a lot of radioactivity!

Nuclear accidents

Very occasionally, things go catastrophically wrong at nuclear power plants. Reactors can overheat and melt down, releasing radiation into the surrounding environment. For example, in 2011, a tsunami flooded a Japanese nuclear power plant, damaging equipment that helped keep the reactors cool. The damage caused the **meltdown** of four reactors. Teams of remote-controlled robots were used to enter the site, which was far too radioactive for humans. Tiny *PackBot* UGV robots inspected for damage and sent a video feed of what their cameras saw. UGVs were mounted with **Geiger counters** to determine the levels of radiation. Larger UGVs with bulldozer blades cleared the rubble. A Toshiba decontamination robot sprayed dry ice at high pressure to scrub off radioactive dust and then sucked up the waste.

Mining

Mining is dangerous work. Miners use powerful machinery to dig out valuable rock, coal, gravel and other heavy materials, and move mined material. They may have to work with explosives or work deep underground where there is risk of tunnel collapse. Each year, thousands of miners are injured as they work. To limit injuries and deaths, the use of robots in the mining industry is increasing.

Giant robot miner

The world's largest robot operates in an open-pit, or surface, coal mine in Australia. This machine weighs 3,448 tonnes (3,800 tons) and stands up to 68.5 metres (225 feet) tall! Its vast bucket drags and scoops up as much as 145 mt (160 t.) of coal at a time. A long arm swings the bucket to where the coal is dumped. Computers coordinate these movements more efficiently and accurately than human operators can.

This is the drill bit at the end of a coal-digging machine.

In China, coal-mining robots operate underground in coal seams. They follow a course guided by laser sensors and their cutting teeth are operated by **remote control** from the surface. Conveyor belts built onto the robot remove the coal it cuts. The robot can even install supports for the tunnels it digs to stop them from caving in.

Investigating mines

Mining robots are also used to investigate abandoned mines. *Groundhog* is a wheeled robot with **laser rangefinders** to view the inner shape of the network of mine tunnels. The data is used to make mine maps. *MOLE* is a tube-shaped robot attached by a cable to the surface, which crawls through narrow tunnels. It has sensors to "sniff out" explosive gases underground, and a video camera to view its surroundings. *MOLE* sends back digital data through the cable so that surface crews can know more about the mine.

Robots are the future

In the future, emergency rescue crews may use robots to rescue coal miners trapped in collapsed tunnels. Rescue crews risk becoming trapped underground while searching for survivors because the tunnels they use may collapse, too. A light robot called *Cheetah-cub* has four legs that move like a cheetah's. It has great balance and a spring in its step to cope with the uneven rocky floor of a partly collapsed tunnel. This robot could deliver life-saving supplies to survivors before a full-scale rescue can be completed.

The *Gasbot* robot has been developed to detect potentially dangerous levels of gas emitted from rotting waste at landfill sites.

31

Chapter 5
Robot inspectors

In many industries there is a need for inspectors to check equipment, machines and materials to ensure they are still working properly or are safe to use. Human inspectors do a lot of checks, but robots are increasingly brought in to make inspections cheaper, quicker and, in some cases, better. Robot inspectors not only have cameras that can take photos or videos, but they also have other sensors, such as **infrared** or sonar, which can be used to see things we cannot see with human eyes.

RailPod *to the rescue*

Inspecting the tracks that trains run on for flaws or problems is a vital part of railway safety. In the past, human inspectors walked the lines but today, in some places, *RailPod* does this job. This robot runs along the railway track using its cameras and sensors to send back data about the track to inspectors at a station. *RailPod* can measure things such as track **alignment**. It can also check the track surface efficiently. This saves time and keeps human workers away from railway tracks, which can be dangerous.

Robots like this carry cameras on board, which film the surrounding areas.

It means human workers can go straight to a location where there is a problem. Autonomous deployment and integrated scheduling allows the railway to inspect the tracks each day.

Structure safety

Large-scale engineering projects can cause terrible damage if they fail. For example, if a dam cracks, it can cause catastrophic floods, power outages and problems for farmers who use the water on their crops. Inspecting the high, steep sides of dams above deep water is tricky and potentially dangerous. In 2013, a new inspection robot successfully climbed the walls of a dam, testing the dam's concrete, checking that it had not cracked or had layers flaking off it, and that any metal attached to it was not rusting. The robot, or crawler bot, has foam-covered tracks and uses **vacuum** suction to suck on to the vertical surface of a dam. Then it follows a pre-programmed route up and down the walls.

Crawler bots suck on to dam walls tightly as they inspect a dam's steep surface.

Crawler bots can carry equipment weighing up to 18 kg (40 lbs.)

33

Wind turbines

Wind **turbines** are impressive feats of engineering. These giant metal windmills that you may see on open stretches of land harness the wind's power and use it to generate electricity. Wind turbines have enormous blades to catch the wind. As the wind blows the blades around, they turn a turbine which makes the electricity. The blades are a vital part of the turbine, but inspecting them can be challenging since they can be 122 m (400 ft.) up in the air. That is where robots come in handy!

Inspector robot

Most inspections of wind turbines are done by humans on the ground, using a telescope or binoculars. Human workers also use climbing equipment to scale the turbine. The former is not very satisfactory and the latter can be dangerous and time-consuming. A robot can do the job much more quickly and safely.

Blade-inspecting robots, such as the HR-MP20, contain powerful magnets. These magnets help the robots cling to metal surfaces so that they can scale a sheer, vertical turbine like a tiny metal Spiderman. They can climb out along the blades, which can be around 61 m (200 ft.) long and about 2.1 m (7 ft.) wide. Even when the turbine is moving in the wind and the robot is right at the end of the blade, the magnets are still powerful enough to stop it being thrown off into the air!

Small but clever

The HR-MP20 robot is just 60.7 centimetres (23.9 inches) wide by 64.8 cm (25.5 in.) deep, and 33.3 cm (13.1 in.) high. Its small size means it is easy for the operator to move it between turbines. The robot is battery-powered, and it can carry up to 9 kilogrammes (20 pounds) of inspection equipment. A human operator controls the robot wirelessly from the ground.

Inspection robots can climb the sheer, vertical trunk of a wind turbine quickly and easily.

Pipe checkers

Beneath our feet there are hundreds of kilometres of pipes carrying water, waste and natural gas. These pipes must be checked regularly to make sure that there are no blockages or things that could contaminate our water supplies. However, checking pipes is a difficult and risky business. Some are very narrow and small, and even though human workers may cover themselves in protective clothing, boots and masks, great care still needs to be taken in larger sewage pipes. Human waste contains **bacteria** and other germs that can cause serious diseases. Not only that, checking sewers is an unpleasant job that few people want to do. This kind of inspection job is ideal for robot inspectors.

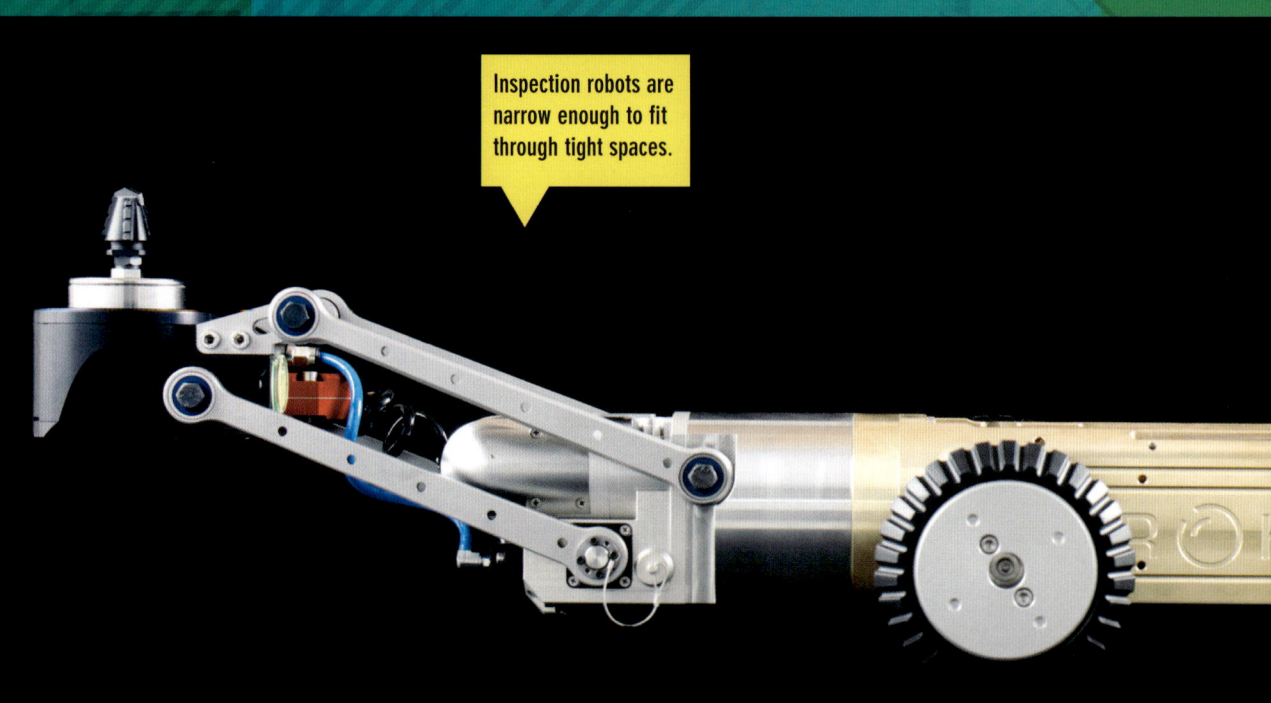

Inspection robots are narrow enough to fit through tight spaces.

Into the pipes

Mobile crawling units inspect some pipes. These units are fitted with CCTV cameras attached to a cable. The newer inspection robots, however, work wirelessly and can carry detection systems that can spot other things, too, such as early stages of rust, which might be missed by doing only a visual check of a sewer or other pipe. To use these robots, a human operator uses a pole and a hook to place the robot into the pipe from above the ground. Then the operator uses a laptop computer to keep track of the robot's location and to give it instructions on where to go. The robot has sensors that help it stay in the centre of a pipe as it trundles along, instead of bumping into the sides, and to avoid falling down holes.

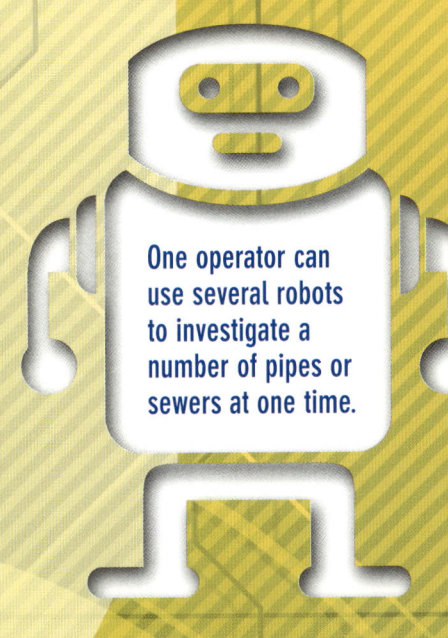

One operator can use several robots to investigate a number of pipes or sewers at one time.

All-seeing and flexible

These battery-operated robots can be equipped with cameras that give a 360-degree view. Many run on six wheels and are completely waterproof so that liquids in the pipes cannot damage them. Some robots have laser rangefinders to measure the width of a pipe and check if it has any dents or collapsed parts. Others have extendable cameras that they can stretch into narrow pipes or around corners to view places that were previously inaccessible.

Chapter 6
Robot farming

People have used machines to help them with the heavy, difficult or time-consuming aspects of farming for many years. Recently, more and more robots have been introduced to the agricultural industry. As in any other industry, farm robots can work faster, longer and more efficiently than human farm workers.

Robots can move between narrow rows of plants, trimming, weeding or spraying plants to keep them healthy.

Weed killers

Robots can be used to do a variety of farming tasks, such as pruning plants, killing weeds and spraying chemicals that kill plant pests or help plants grow. One prototype that has been developed is for a robot that kills weeds as it moves slowly across rows of lettuce plants in a field. As it moves along, the robot compares images of the plants it sees with an on-board database of more than one million images of plants. If it finds a weed, it sprays a strong dose of **fertilizer** over the weed. This burns and kills the weed, which then soaks into the soil to help the lettuce grow!

Nursery workers

Some robots work in plant nurseries, which are places where young plants and trees are grown for sale or for planting elsewhere. *Harvey* is an autonomous robot that moves around the plant nursery, identifying which plants have grown so much that they are getting too close together. The robots can also move plants around when it is time to send them off for planting. These robots move along on tyres, and use gripper arms and trays to do their work. A human operator inputs plant locations on a touchscreen grid and the robot uses sensors to locate, pick up and move the potted plants.

The HV-100 robot works in plant nurseries and greenhouses, lifting and moving plant pots of different sizes.

Robots are the future

By 2050, we will need to produce about 70 per cent more food than we do today to feed the world's growing population. Robot farmers could help us with this because they help human farmers produce more food, more quickly.

Robot farmers

Farmers have to take care of fruit and vegetable crops to make sure they produce a harvest. It takes a lot of time to collect or pick the food they produce. Robots can help with all these jobs.

The *Agrobot* looks cumbersome, but its robotic arms can analyse each strawberry before cutting and picking the fruit.

Robots do the gardening

Fruit and vegetable plants need a lot of tending to keep them healthy. For example, in vineyards, grapevines must be trimmed, or pruned, to keep them healthy. This is a time-consuming job when you have a huge vineyard, so inventors have come up with a prototype for a robot that can do this job. This robot has four wheels, a pair of arms and six cameras, and it can prune 600 vines per day. It uses the cameras to guide its two arms with clippers at the ends, and it has tracking technology and on-board maps to help it move from vine to vine. Some of the cameras store the shape of each vine so that the robot can use a 3D model to know when each plant should be pruned and by how much.

Harvest time

Some robots help with picking or harvesting fruit and vegetables. The challenge for robots like this is to handle the produce with care, so as not to damage or bruise it, making it unsaleable. The ACRO automated fruit-picking machine (AFPM) is attached to the back of a tractor, and it has a tool at the end of its robot arm that picks apples with great precision and care. It uses a flexible cone to pull the fruit off the tree using vacuum suction. The end of the arm has a camera inside so it can see the exact shape of each apple it picks. The amazing thing about this robot is that it can also tell from the colour of the apple if it is ripe or not, and therefore whether or not it should pick the apple!

Ripe and robot ready!

A robot strawberry picker can also tell from the colour of the fruit whether it is ripe and ready to pick. After checking that the fruit is ripe using its digital cameras, a robotic arm reaches out and snips a strawberry free from its parent plant. It then places it in a collection basket. This strawberry-picking robot is about 2 m (6 ft.) tall and it moves between rows of strawberries in greenhouses on a system of rails.

Agrobots can select strawberries based on their size, quality and ripeness.

Robomilk!

Milking cows is hard work for a dairy farmer. Farmers have to get up early in the morning and then go out for hours in the evening every single day, whatever the weather, to gather up their herd of cows, take them to the milking parlour and attach them to machines that extract the milk. New robotic milking machines give dairy farmers new-found freedom and the time to do other necessary farmwork.

All-day milking parlour

A great advantage of robotic milking machines is that cows can visit them whenever they like, even in the middle of the night. They walk into the milking parlour because they know that there is food waiting for them there. Once inside, a laser-guided robot arm is triggered into action. This locates each of the cow's **teats**, cleans it and attaches a milking tube to it. A sensor checks that the milk is clean and safe to drink and will "spit" out any milk that is not. The machine continues to take milk until the flow slows down. Then the machine releases the tubes and the cow leaves.

Passing on data

The system works because the cows wear **transponders** around their necks. Transponders are devices that receive and **transmit radio signals**. These connect to the computers in the robot milking machine, so it knows which cow is which. The machine scans each cow's underside with lasers, and links to a computer that records data about each cow and their milking habits. This allows the farmer to keep an eye on his herd by checking data that is uploaded from the robot. The data tells the farmer when each cow was last milked, how often it visited the milking parlour, how much it ate and how much milk each cow produced.

Robotic milking machines can help farmers produce more milk and keep their prices competitive.

Robots are the future

Another job that can be tricky for a dairy farmer is rounding up a large herd of cattle. In the future, robots might do this, too. Inventors are working on a robot that could round up cows like a farm dog. It will use **GPS** and sensors to gather cows together and march them slowly to where the farmer wants them to go.

Farm watch

Walking through giant fields to check on crops as they grow is a job that every farmer would like to do, but few have the time. So, many farmers are starting to use **drones** – flying robots – first used by the army, to help them do this job.

Farm drones

Drones are unmanned **aerial vehicles (UAVs)** that look like little planes or helicopters. To launch them, farmers throw them into the air. The drones can carry different types of cameras and equipment, such as **thermal imagers**, to collect pictures and information that farmers could not see with the naked eye. The data tells farmers many things, such as where patches of soil are too wet or too dry, where plants are looking sickly because insects are eating them, or which crops need fertilizer to help them grow bigger. Using drones can save farmers money because they can apply things such as **pesticides** only where needed and not over entire fields.

Drones are easy to operate using a simple handset device.

Drones like this are just one kind of robot we will be seeing more of on farms in the future!

Drones can even tell farmers if livestock are unwell because thermal imagers show differences in temperature. Sick animals are slightly warmer than healthy ones.

Industrial robots in the future

Advances in technology and electronics mean that robots are becoming more and more intelligent every year, and new, more autonomous robots are working in farming and other industries all the time. Today, factory robots have limitations. Most have to be programmed by humans to perform a simple task, which they then simply repeat again and again. However, as robot technology improves, maybe one day it could be the robots and not the humans who are making decisions and being creative in jobs across different industries?

Robots are the future

There are already prototypes for a driverless tractor that has no need of a cab for a farmer to sit in, and runs on caterpillar tracks. Farmers will be able to control it from a base station or with a portable controller, and they can have a number of tractors working their fields at the same time! The tractor avoids obstacles using a combination of computers, lasers and radio signals and can have different tools, such as ploughs, attached to the back of it, just like any normal tractor.

Glossary

aerial in the air

alignment when something is in alignment, its parts are in a straight line

autonomous able to act on its own, without outside control

bacteria tiny living things that exist everywhere in nature; some bacteria can cause disease

barcode set of thick and thin lines placed on a product that give a computer information about it

cancer serious disease

caterpillar track metal band that moves around the wheels of a vehicle to help it move across rough ground

CCTV (stands for closed-circuit television) use of video cameras to send images to a specific place or monitor

circuit board thin, rigid board containing a series of electric circuits that control a computer's functions

component part

contaminated unfit for use because of contact with a harmful substance

conveyor belt continuously moving band that is used for transporting objects from one place to another

corrosion process of being broken down by a chemical process

drone robot aircraft

electrode part that passes electricity in and out

end effector device at the end of a robotic arm

exoskeleton rigid external covering for the body

fertilizer substance that is used to help plants grow bigger or better

flammable capable of catching fire easily

Geiger counter device that detects radioactivity

GPS (stands for Global Positioning System) electronic tool used to find the exact location of an object

humanoid shaped like a human

hydraulic powered by fluid forced through pipes or chambers

infrared rays of light that cannot be seen by human eyes

joint place where two things or parts, such as bones, are joined

laser very narrow beam of highly concentrated light

laser rangefinder device that uses lasers to judge distance

lethal deadly

meltdown severe nuclear reactor accident that results from overheating

missile object that is thrown or launched as a weapon towards a target

nitrogen gas that has no colour or smell and that is found in the atmosphere

pallet movable platform on which heavy loads are stacked

pesticide chemical used to kill insects and fungi that can damage plants

pollution harmful materials that damage the air, water and soil

pressure force that pushes or pulls something

production line line of machines, equipment and workers in a factory that makes a product by working on it and passing it on to the next workstation until it is finished

productivity number of products produced

prototype first working model of a new invention

radiation rays of energy given off by radioactive elements

radio signal message sent on invisible radiowaves through the air

reactor device for the controlled release of nuclear energy

remote control operating a machine from a distance

scan read data for use by a computer

sensor device that detects changes such as heat or movement

silicon chip small piece of silicon that is used in computers, calculators and other electronic devices

simulation software 3D computer model of a situation or place

stationary not moving

teat part of a female animal through which a baby animal drinks milk

thermal imager device that makes images of things by sensing the heat they give off

transmit to send out signals

transponder device for transmitting and receiving signals

turbine machine with blades that can generate electricity

vacuum empty space from which all the air has been sucked out

Find out more

Books
Everything Robotics, Jennifer Swanson (National Geographic Kids, 2016)

Producing Dairy and Eggs (The Technology of Farming), Jane Bingham (Raintree, 2013)

Robots and the Whole Technology Story (Science Sorted), Glenn Murphy (Macmillan Children's Books, 2015)

Websites
Watch car robots at work at:
www.bbc.co.uk/programmes/p011mw4v

Watch this video of cows being milked by robotic milking machines:
www.thisisdairyfarming.com/discover/watch/robotic-milking

Find out about all kinds of engineers and what they do at:
www.tomorrowsengineers.org.uk

Index

ACRO automated fruit-picking machine (AFPM) 41
Agrobots 40, 41
aeroplanes 10, 11
arms 6–7, 8, 9, 11, 12, 13, 14, 16, 17, 20, 25, 26, 27, 29, 30, 39, 40, 41, 42
army 44
assembly line 5, 10, 15, 16
automated guided vehicles (AGVs) 25
autonomous remote vehicles (ARVs) 27
AutoStore 22, 23
aviation industry 9

barcode 18, 21
Baxter 17
Boeing 11

cameras 15, 19, 29, 31, 32, 37, 41, 44
Cartesian robot 6
caterpillar tracks 27, 45
chemicals 10, 14, 26, 27, 39
clippers 41
closed-circuit television (CCTV) 19, 37
computers 9, 14, 15, 17, 18, 19, 21, 25, 30, 37, 42, 45
conveyor belts 5, 17, 18, 19, 20, 24, 25, 30
crawler bots 33

dams 33
distribution 24–25
drones 44, 45
drugs 9

electricity 12, 28, 34
Equipois X-Ar 17

exoskeleton 17
explosions 26

factories 4, 5, 8, 9, 11, 12, 13, 15, 25, 26, 45
farmers 33, 39, 40–41, 42, 43, 44, 45
farming 9, 38–45
fertilizer 39, 44
finishing 16–17
food industry 9
Ford, Henry 10
fruit 24, 40, 41

Gasbot 31
gases 31
Geiger counters 29
General Motors 4
GPS (Global Positioning System) 43
gripping tools 7
Groundhog 31

Harvey 39
HR-MP20 34, 35
humanoid 17
HV-100 39
hydraulics 6

inspectors 32–37

Kiva 20, 21

lasers 13, 25, 30, 31, 37, 42, 45
livestock 45

mining 30–31
MOLE 31
motors 6

nuclear power 28–29
nuclear waste 28, 29

PackBot 29
paint 8, 11, 14, 15
painting 14–15
pesticides 44
pharmaceutical industry 9, 22
pickers 20–21, 41
pipes 14, 29, 36–37
plant nurseries 39
production line 5
protective clothing 12, 36
Python 6

radiation 28, 29
RailPod 32
railways 32, 33
rangefinders 31, 37

safety 32, 33
sensors 8, 17, 21, 27, 23, 30, 31, 32, 37, 39, 42, 43
silicon 9
software 15, 19, 20
SwissLog Click&Pick 23

termite-bots 27
tyres 16, 39
tractors 41, 45

Unimate 4
unmanned aerial vehicles (UAVs) 44
unmanned ground vehicle (UGV) 29

vegetables 24, 40, 41
vehicles 4, 8, 9, 10, 14, 15, 16

warehouses 18–25, 26
welding 7, 12–13
wheels 16, 23, 27, 37, 41
wind turbines 34–35